The Truth About Drugs and Teens:

An Informed Perspective

By: Jessica Lohman

authorHOUSE™

1663 LIBERTY DRIVE, SUITE 200
BLOOMINGTON, INDIANA 47403
(800) 839-8640
WWW.AUTHORHOUSE.COM

First published by AuthorHouse 12/02/05

ISBN: 1-4208-9401-3 (sc)

Library of Congress Control Number: 2005909411

Printed in the United States of America
Bloomington, Indiana

This book is printed on acid-free paper.

Acknowledgements

The information in this book is derived from thousands of newspaper articles, college classes, books, documentaries, interviews with drug addicts and former drug users, medical personnel, internet research, conferences, training, seminars, doctors, psychologists, magazines, and events I have experienced personally. I am not taking credit for the countless hours of work hundreds of people have done to supply the information presented in this book. As it was impossible to quote every source from my entire college education, a heartfelt thanks is deserved to the work invested to aid the movement for younger generations to have a better life.

Table of Contents

FORWARD - DRUG ESSAYS
BY TEENS IN JUVENILE HALL

When I began my career, I worked in a Juvenile Hall correctional facility located in northern California. As the teenage residents would misbehave, rather than send them to their rooms for hours, I requested they write me a one page essay on any subject of my choice. On topics pertaining to drugs, it was touching to see the depth of some of the wards and to read of their experiences from home written on paper. It was astonishing to see the numerous mistakes and the poor writing skills of teenagers who would have otherwise been in high school. It became evident that these teenagers had little knowledge about the facts of illegal drugs. This motivated me to educate myself about all kinds of narcotics so I could share the truth with them. Although the names have been changed for confidentiality purposes, the following are real essays and statements that were written in Juvenile Hall by the teens who lived there. All of the errors are authentic:

Why shouldn't teens use drugs?

Teens shouldn't use drugs because it is really bad for tem ad their lungs get all bad and out of shape. - Curtis, Age 16.

Why Shouldn't Teenagers Experiment with Drugs?

The reason why teenagers shouldn't experiment with drugs is because the [they] might do something stupid and kill somebody or really hurt some body very badly. Another reason why teenagers shouldn't use drugs is because you might strung out or hooked on it. Another reason why teenager's shouldn't do drugs is because they might over dose. Another reason why teenager's shouldn't use drugs is because they might get skinny and be poor because and spent all there money up on drugs and they might end up in jail for possession of drugs and might start acting different and they might end up doing stuff they don't want to but the must steal or kill somebody to get the money to buy the Drugs and another reason is because they will steal anything to sell to get the drugs. Another reason why they shouldn't be experimenting with drugs is because they have a full future in front of them. Another reason is because it takes away their worries and tricks them into thinking that there are better off high and not realizing that it makes them dummer [dumber] in the long run. Plus they destroy they brain cells for a 30 minute high. That is why teenagers experiment with drugs because of curiosity. -Paul, Age 16.

Drugs

People shouldn't use drugs because it messes up their personalitiy [personality], image, and self asteam [esteem], like lets say for instance a young man use drug hes goin to hert [hurt] himself do bodily damage But hes not just herting himself es herting his parents and other relatives But drugs also messe up people's futer [future] like (Dope) it makes your nose clog up bleed and other things (Weed) it fries the hell out of your Brain sells makes you have short term memories (hairon) [heroin] it kills your vein you can catch hepatitis, AiDS, and overdose you can also get a bad reputation like if you buy drugs everyone's gona know that you do it and their going to laugh at you and you going to be talk of the town alcool [alcohol] to my egnologment [acknowledgement] kills your liver it makes you soft you could get a Dui [DUI-driving under the influence] you could also kill people like car accidents they are the most popolar [popular] accidents. The end. - Todd, Age 15.

Why Shouldn't Teens

Prohibition has failed again it has long been clear that the laws on Drugs are Doing more harm than good for understandable reason governments and voters alike are reluctant to face the facts. The case for legalisation is strong both in principle and as a practical matter Leader the law Don't work a survey.

And I think the people that smoke or Do Drugs can be often harmfull specly [especially] teenager my age see I will be 15 October 3. Drugs will keep you out of school and is harmful to the head and I Don't know the treatment for the help that they give for your head. It may even make you loco like me.- Vincent, Age 14.

Why shouldn't teenager experiment with drugs?

I think they think is kool or they wanted to fix in with there friends. Drugs are bad because it could cost your life and also you could go to jail for using or selling drugs. Peoples thinks drugs calm them down but, no drugs just make you friend more and it could also kill you. Drugs the most dangerous things that peoples use. Lots of the teenager in high school use drugs likes smoking at school and selling drugs to younger kids. Drugs are used to make people buy more and more.

[No Title]

Teenager should not use drug because it could affect your health and loses all you money. It would bad If you use to many drugs and how are you going to pay your bills, and also cost you a lot s of money for a car. Teen should know how drugs is doing to affect there life and it might affect there future. There won't be no girls that going to marry them.

Drugs can make you loses brain cell you won't remember anything what you did it won't make you stupid and can read or write. It'll make you so stupid you have to go through Pre-school again. This is why teenager shouldn't use drugs. Kelby, Age 16.

[No Title]

When your talking to kids about drugs a good way to talk about it is telling them the risk of doing drugs. For example, when you are selling drugs you could get robbed or shot or sometimes you could even die. Another thing you could told to them about is what could happen to you in the long run. Most times people lose the jobs, family, friends, and most times even their lives. Then you talk to them about how good life would be without drugs. - Marey, Age 17.

Why Teenager's Shoud [Should] not use Drugs.

Teenagers shoud not use drugs because it mesies [messes] up their life. When you smoke weeD it kills the brain sells in your body. When you Do eny [any] Meith infediamy [methaphetamine] is eats your body and mesies up your life. When your adickted [addicted] to drugs it is hard to get out, I hade to go though [through] it myself. I used to smoke weed and sell it to. I used to sell almost every drug out there right now. I wish I hade never of don it but ever sense I took one puff of the week I never stoped untill now. Now I don't smoke weed I don't smoke enything [anything]. I don't sell eney kind of drug ethier [either]. I used to drink Beer too, but I stoped that real quik [quick]. but I just moved last mounth [month] and I'v bin [been] sober for three in a half mounths. I changed my friends and now I have no friend that smoke sigarets [cigarettes] - smoke weed or drink beer. I see my old friends one's [once] in awioll [a while] but there look all srubed up. And a lot of them are locked up and some of theme are even in prison to. I even now *[know], some people that are in there [their] thirty's and fourtey's that still Do drugs and still sell drugs and drink ber to. But they are a real bad exsampal [example] to me and, all teenagers to. I wish I never would of took that first hit of weed and that first drink of beer because [because] I probley [probably] would not be in the sichuwashun [situation] I am in now. I probley would never be on probashan [probation] or most of the policy [police] would not now [know] me. Mostly all the crime Iv [I've] done was under the influence of alchahol or marrimona [marijuana]. Last year when I went to school I always used to skip school just to go smoke and drink I got bad grades and got suspended all the time. And it was all because of drugs. I probley got about twenty brain cell's. But I can still tink that's why I don't smoke and don't brink [drink]- It ant [ain't] worth the consiqens [consequences] is ant worth the time. Prity [pretty] mutch [much] smocking weed or doing eny other tipe [type] of druge or drinking prity mutch meses up your life. It gets you now were [nowhere] and you ethier [either] are on the streets with no money or in a jail sell with nothing at all but some close [clothes] and a bed. Well I writen my esay and her it is. - Sam, Age 17.*

After viewing these chilling reflections and interesting points of view, I hope you are ready to look at the truth of the relationship between illegal drugs and young people. The following chapters contain the information I discovered while conducting my research about various substances. My research provided me with the ability to share, through factual information, with teenage criminals the reality of their choices. As I began to tell these teens about the risks associated with drugs, a miraculous thing took place. I witnessed them change their lives and belief systems for the better. For the first time someone cared to spend the time with them on an individual basis. For the first time research was done by an adult they knew on *their* behalf for the purpose of answering *their* questions. I am encouraged they were able to change their lives for the better as many were not involved with the Criminal Justice System after that time.

It was during that time I realized that not only could this information assist and encourage kids involved in the Juvenile Justice System, but all teens who were curious and needed real answers. Additionally, the material would be beneficial to the parents of these minors, professionals involved in education, mental health practitioners, social workers, and law enforcement. As a service to all of these parties, this book is designed to be a source of reference based on one persons experiences on how drugs impact the lives of teens.

CHAPTER 1 - SETTING THE RECORD STRAIGHT ABOUT DRUGS

The use of legal and illegal drugs can be detected in the history, recreation and habits of generations both present and past. Contributing factors include cultural traditions of past ancestors, religious significance, creativity, inspiration, or a desire for antisocial connotation. For some these substances are traditions of past ancestors, for others may have a religious significance, and still others may find a creative or antisocial connotation to be associated with such use. Some consider these practices dangerous while others believe it to be harmless. Pertaining to this conflict, many individuals on both sides of the spectrum are unable to articulate clear reasoning and therefore fact and opinion become blended into confusion.

Young people have embraced the drug world as a means of rebellion and defiance, trying to create their own legacy while at the same time surpassing that of the previous generation. Currently, many teens have grown up in environments where drug use is considered to be a normality and not of great significance. Passively, this attitude reinforces acceptance in self medicating for the purpose of coping with traumatic and stressful situations. These teens who lack support and reasoning to develop strong convictions against drug use tend to fall subject to its appeal at an early age. During the past decade, many of these youth participate in the drug culture through 'Raves.'

Consider in your own mind what the definition of a Rave might be. There might be intense strobe light shows, people dressed extravagantly in costume apparel such as high shoes and perhaps some wings on their back, glow in the dark beads, glow sticks, pacifiers, people in your face, "You rollin'?," a multitude of ages, expensive bottled water, varieties of loud, energetic music, aliases, and striptease dancers. Overall, the definition of a *Rave* could be summed up in this collaboration: An all-night party containing impressive lighting and music which caters to early teens and young adults where a wide variety of controlled substances are available.

Sounds fun and exciting, if it weren't for the vicious realities associated with Raves. There are a multitude of undercover cops and media, many of whom have secret cameras taking footage of events, people, and drug sales. Kids under the influence of drugs over heat and pass out. When a teen does lose consciousness, the so-called friends disappear almost immediately because they are afraid of being involved. This is a terrifying concept, that at the most vulnerable moment these teens have no consistent support. Additionally, security personnel drag the victims into alleyways or out to the parking lot and leave them unattended and vulnerable to further victimization. Random teens freak out for no apparent reason - half awake and half dreaming, there is footage of them dropping and screaming at their own apparent hallucinations. One of the most terrifying recollections of a Rave include someone randomly injecting people with syringes of blood in the darkness amongst the crowd. Attached to these syringes were notes reading "Welcome to the world of AIDS." Luckily, no one tested positive for HIV, however, this is an important illustration of the risk of attending Raves and being associated with people who do. These occurrences are factual and are not rumors. Fortunately, there has been a recent decrease in Rave participation and therefore such occurrences are happening less frequently. Apparently, many have

come to the conclusion that ultimately a Rave is just the place to be

if you want to hinder your full potential, and the whole point of this

thing we call "life."

CHAPTER 2 - ALCOHOL: MOST CONVENIENT, MOST DESTRUCTIVE

The greatest people alive are lost to alcohol. Loved ones suffer gravely are a result of it's irresponsible consumption. It gives birth to confusion, forgetfulness, addiction, and hardships.

At a party when I was in college, we were amongst a few dozen friends and at some point in the evening a random girl showed up who lived in the neighborhood. No one knew her so no one paid particular attention to her. She drank excessively, but she remained unnoticed as the party guests socialized, danced, and entertained one another. While inebriated, this girl found her way into a Jacuzzi in the back yard. After hearing a great deal of commotion, we went outside to determine its source. This girl sat in the corner of the Jacuzzi with her eyes closed, exposing herself to the crowd while rubbing her body in the bubbles. Alarmingly, she appeared to be passing in and out of consciousness. It is common knowledge that alcohol consumption and warm places do not go hand in hand, so we attempted to reason with her to get her out of the Jacuzzi. The girl declined, and turned to a group of guys observing her display and declared that she would sleep with all of them if they would keep her in the Jacuzzi. They honorably did not comply with her request and assisted in removing her from the Jacuzzi. We carried her into the house, covered her up, and attempted to dry her off. She told us to call a friend to come get her but did not have the number, luckily it was quickly located in her purse. Her friend was contacted, and she was taken safely home. The frightening aspect of this incident is that this girl irresponsibly entrusted her life to a bunch of rowdy, partying college kids. A situation where she could have been severely taken advantage of or possibly even killed. Yet that is the disillusioned reality of alcohol.

It is easy to become addicted to alcohol, and unfortunately hundreds of people do. Any brief search on the Internet will reveal the common statistic that every one (1) in five (5) people suffer from alcoholism as its the easiest substance to fall victim to. Take a moment to think of someone in your family who has an alcohol related problem. Many people I have known began consuming alcohol before age twenty-one. If your experience has been anything like mine, you probably know people who had an incredible potential to do something magnificent. However, do to alcoholism, many of the people are stuck in monotonous, dead end jobs and living resentful lives. When I reflect on the lives of family and friends who have created this life for themselves, I am saddened because I can imagine all of the incredible accomplishments they could have made if they had not been sucked into that addiction.

Every fifteen minutes in the United States an accident happens in which an alcohol related death occurs. That is a substantial and unnecessary loss of life due to blatant irresponsibility. Alcohol is societies temporary band-aid to console the troubled, but there are always consequences to drinking for teens as well as adults. The hang over the next morning, laziness at work, dehydration, and a lack of motivation to accomplish daily tasks frequently accompanies the use of alcohol. Long term use of alcohol leads to cirrhosis of the liver, pancreatitis, strokes, and cancer.

Often times, kids tell me of times they have ingested alcohol with another substance; however, they have no idea the consequences of their actions. Often times this can result in a severe heart or liver damage. It literally shocks the system. Alcohol effects every part of the body, but causes different reactions in different people. It can cause a range of emotional responses, causing one person to relax and the other to become extremely aggressive and violent.

An increasingly alarming trend, is the number of adults who are providing youth with alcohol. Parents, often believe in the concept of creating a safe environment for their children to drink "responsibly." So they purchase alcohol and allow children to come over and drink in a controlled environment. However, there are a few problems with this. Firstly, it encourages adults providing to youth and teaches their children to copy the same behavior when they become parents dealing with the same frustrations of alcohol with their own children. Secondly, these same parents are viewed more as friends than parents, so their children do not take them seriously and tend to avoid going to their parents with critical problems. Thirdly, these parents or adults either drink to the point of intoxication with their guests or try to make themselves scarce so as to not infringe on the reputation of their child. If an adult is drinking their ability to handle emergency situations with a clear head will be hindered. Additionally, the fear of getting busted prohibits them from guaranteeing a person in need will get the adequate care they may require. Fourthly, providing alcohol to a minor is contributing to their delinquency and is a violation of the law.

According to the Substance Abuse and Mental Health Services Administration, 2,600,000 teens are oblivious to the fact that a person can die from alcohol use. Obviously, I am going to recommend that everyone steer clear of this stuff, and I will also remind that it is illegal to drink alcohol until age twenty-one in the United States. I am not condoning the use of alcohol in any way and those who avoid it until they are of legal age are beautiful examples of being a good influence on humanity. I do understand, however, that some people possess active curiosity despite all attempts to dissuade from experimenting with alcohol. A high school student attending an occasional party or graduating from high school and progressing to college may honestly benefit from referring to the tips for drinking located in the chapter entitled *Ecstasy's Right Hand Drug.* Those tips just might save your life.

"Who has woe? Who has sorrow?
Who has strife? Who has complaints?
Who has needless bruises? Who has bloodshot eyes?

Those who linger over wine
who go to sample bowls of mixed wine.

Do not gaze at wine when it red,
when it sparkles in the cup,
when it goes down smoothly!

In the end it bites like a snake
And poisons like a viper."

-Proverbs 23:29-32

CHAPTER 3 - DID YOU INHALE?

Marijuana - Pot - Grass - Mary Jane - Reefer - Sensimilla - Cannabis - Hemp - Bud - a green, leafy-looking plant which is illegal in the United States and a multitude of other places. It has been my experience that most people do not know what it actually does to the body. When I ask a roomful of students to raise their hand if marijuana isn't that bad for you, half the students raise their hands. Additionally, when I ask how many people think marijuana is really bad for you, only half the students raise their hands. "Well why or why not?" I ask them .

"Marijauna is medicine!"

"Marijuana puts holes in your brain!"

"My Dad smoked marijuana when he was in college and he's just fine!"

"My Uncle smokes it and he's really messed up!"

"My buddy can't get a hard on since he started smoking it!"

These are the responses derived from the voices of a multitude of backgrounds. So is pot actually unhealthy for you or isn't it?

The majority of the parents of today's young people smoked it and they appear to be productive members of society. Although this paints a confusing picture for today's youth, this fact does not have much validity because marijuana is a completely different substance now than it was then. For example, the potency of one (1) joint today is equal to fourteen (14) joints from the 1960's.

Marijuana has a dangerous chemical in its ingredients concerning which there is a great deal of commotion about known as delta-9-tetrahydrocannibinol (THC), yet the majority of the population does not know what it does. THC is the single most potent chemical in marijuana. It is the chemical that allows a person to get high, get silly, get hungry, and get stupid. It also does the most amount of damage to the body of any other chemical in marijuana.

If a teen were to go out and buy a random bag of marijuana in the 1960's, there would be less than 1% THC in any given variety. Marijauna-growing operators discovered they could increase the THC level by breeding the hybrids. Various marijuana producers became competitive and by the 1970's, the THC level had increased by 5%. It is no secret that people who grow marijuana make a lot of money. So they didn't stop there.

By the 1980's, the approximate THC level fluctuated around 10%. This was the first time in history that people voluntarily began to check themselves into rehabilitation programs. It was the first time in history people struggled to maintain a decently balanced life while smoking marijuana on a regular basis. People were breaking out into sweats in the shower, having difficulty with basic life skills such as sleeping, arriving to work on time, concentrating for any length of time, accomplishing menial tasks, getting an erection, maintaining a sex drive, keeping their house in a decent order, and remembering how to cook certain meals. It was the first time in history people were unable to quit smoking marijauna on their own. They had cravings. Many people say marijuana is not addictive. I would encourage them to explain why thousands upon thousands of Americans could not quit on their own initiative. How can marijuana not be habit-forming addictive if they experienced "cravings?"

By the 1990's, smoking marijuana had developed a very negative connotation with the assistance of the "Just Say 'NO!'" political campaign and those who chose marijuana anyway were exposed to approximately 15% THC. Currently, law enforcement is making a valiant effort eradicating marijuana growing operations. As a result, the marijuana market took on a new trend. Although some is still grown locally, much is shipped and trafficked in from other places and countries. Interesting, is that marijuana operations are Alaska's number one crop according to several newspapers who took actual photographs of underground operations!

The bottom line is the supply will always be here, the demand is the only control we have. If there was no demand, there would be no market and therefore no purpose for mass amounts of drug supplies would exist. Today the average THC level in any given variety of marijuana currently lands at an approximate 40%. That fact is almost unbelievable. That is darn near half a joint. Now the question becomes, "What does THC actually do?"

Most people are familiar with how marijuana is used. Marijuana is generally smoked. Unless the user is on a baking kick and make some brownies or something. Yet marijuana users tend to be on the lazy side so ganja brownies are infrequent. Most frequently, however, the individual inhales the substance- the air travels down the trachea- the lungs expand, and it is absorbed into the blood stream the same way oxygen is. Via the blood stream, the chemicals are transferred through the body to the brain which makes it possible for all the effects to take place. THC is recognized by the brain to be a neurotransmitter called anandomide (an element of the limbic system). A neurotransmitter is what I call a "pleasure juice," or a series of chemicals which are released by the brain which make you feel good.

Unfortunately, THC is not anandomide. It is not even a neurotransmitter but rather a toxic poison that resembles one. So the brain readily accepts the THC because it falsely registers as a neurotransmitter. Therefore the brain makes itself vulnerable and THC is able to cause brain damage. This is where the rumor, "It makes holes in your brain," comes into play. It just might. THC certainly causes brain damage that creates permanent new patterns in the way the brain operates.

Additionally, THC is biologically active. The term biologically active means that the THC manipulates the cells of the body at a microscopic level. So as already stated, marijuana is usually smoked and the transportation system is the bloodstream. As the bloodstream comes in contact with body cells, the question becomes, "What part of the body doesn't the blood stream touch?" Considering all of the places the bloodstream touches in the body, it might be more effective to identify the places it doesn't, and hair and fingernails sum that up. Although if you rip your hair and fingernails out, it will probably bleed, correct? Toe nails work the same way. Therefore, as THC is biologically active, the THC mutates each cell it comes in contact with. When the THC mutates a cell, and that cell multiplies (as cells do), then you have a mutated cell that has been multiplied, which continue to multiply. This multiplication of mutated cells can become a deadly disease known as cancer. Some people would argue that they are going to die someday anyway so they may as well have fun while they are alive. My counter argument is that it might be helpful not to enhance the potential of a painful, prolonged ordeal which pulls yourself and your family through much heartache. To live a healthy life is the responsible thing to do for yourself. Would you rather be the 78 year old marathon runner or the 60 year old newly retired, wheeling your oxygen tank around, cancer patient?

THC is only one of 360 chemicals in marijuana. However, that number does not stay 360. Although the brain does not recognize THC as a poison, the liver does, and it works to purge it from the system. During the purging process, the THC is altered into 60 new chemicals. Therefore it might be fair to say that marijuana results in a total 420 chemicals. That is a scary concept. Even foot powder only has five chemicals and thankfully no one smokes that.

Marijuana interferes with experiencing emotions, motor coordination, short term memory, and your heart rate. Lots of people need help with their short term memory as it is. Although some of the appeals of marijuana are that it provides the user with an illusion of acceptance, relaxation, happiness, and the ability to make choices conscience-free (for example, having sex with someone you normally wouldn't), using marijuana does not actually change a life for the better. It is a temporary mirage and at the end of the high a person is still the person they were beforehand. Using marijuana puts a priceless person at risk of being put in harms way. Mildly, side effects include blood shot eyes, dry mouth, time alteration, and weight gain, yet more common is the inability to complete complex tasks, using poor judgment which increases harmful decisions, and the lack of motivation. Marijuana smokers tend to be lazy and have no goals or desire to become better people.

A common joke amongst the college population is most pot smokers are on the nine year plan to accomplish a Bachelor's Degree (a four year accomplishment). Of the several pot smokers I knew from college, very few of them ever graduated. Evidently, marijuana use wastes important time and hinders the potential of an otherwise successful population. Although this opinion may not be popular, acquaintances who have been busted or have sought treatment are in agreement with me.

Marijuana use can be an extremely dangerous threat to the safety of children. Five toddlers were recently admitted into an emergency room for cannabis poisoning. Of course they did not smoke it, they were merely exposed to the marijuana, due to the impaired judgment on behalf of the parents. The San Francisco Chronicle has published articles about how the use of marijuana impairs the brain of a child.

The serious side effects of marijuana use include cognition, paranoia, acute anxiety reaction (a psychotic breakdown), post-traumatic perception disorder, acute and chronic bronchitis, and deficiency to the immune system. Many students I have worked with, have experienced these symptoms, and had to watch their family members suffer with them. If you have ever had bronchitis, you can imagine having it permanently because marijuana destroys the filters in your lungs. Stephen Covey wrote an excellent book entitled *Principle Centered Leadership* in which he states, that "to put anything harmful in the body is foolishness". A stroke of genius balanced on a bridge of common sense.

When people make a habit of using marijuana, attempting to quit can be difficult. Professionals in the field regularly encounter their caseload suffering from the following withdrawal symptoms: Anger, irritability, aches, pains, chills, depression, an inability to concentrate, sleep disturbances, sweating, and cravings.

When your friends or acquaintances are entertaining ideas of using or are currently use this substance, step up to the challenge and invite them over to talk to them about it. Inform them of the risks associated with its use. You can make a huge difference in the lives of others who may otherwise wind up suffering drastically from such choices. It is certainly not easy, and is extremely courageous. I honor the positive efforts made on behalf of you and your community members.

CHAPTER 4 - COLD HEARTED METHAMPHETAMINE

Here is a poster child for the reality of methamphetamine.

Maria is a beautiful 3-year old. She has long wavy hair and big brown eyes. Her favorite activity is rolling down big grassy hills and it truly warms your heart to hear her laugh. Unfortunately for Maria, her mother was arrested for manufacturing methamphetamine at their residence in Oregon. At the time of her mother's arrest, Maria was taken into custody by Child Protective Services (CPS). Her mother was sentenced to nine years in prison with enhancements for manufacturing in the presence of a minor.

As a result, Maria was facing adoption and permanent foster care. It was a sad time in her life. Just when she left completely abandoned and alone, Maria's Aunt and Uncle stepped forward and stated they would be willing to take custody of the child. This was a huge sacrifice for them as anyone who has ever had an exchange student live with them or had family come visit can understand that with another person comes a good deal of responsibility. It means extra towels for the shower, additional loads of laundry, extra food preparation, scheduling shower times and so on and so forth, let alone accepting a dependant 3-year old into the home. CPS was glad to keep Maria in the scope of her loving relatives to promote family reunification. Before long, all the arrangements were made and she had been adopted.

The problem with Maria's new home is her Aunt and Uncle are methamphtamine users too. Maria doesn't laugh so much anymore. When she has temper tantrums as 3-years olds do, her aunt and uncle put a hanger in the back of her shirt and hang her in the closet for hours. If Maria is still crying when they come back to check on her they leave her in the closet all night or take her out and stuff her into a small box. And Maria's beautiful face, as well as her arms and legs, are covered with cigarette burns which have been inflicted for punishment.

You might be wondering to yourself if this story has a happy ending. Truth be told, it has a horrifying ending. After being tortured for days, Maria died screaming while her own family held her in a pot of boiling water while they were under the influence of methamphetamine. It may be one thing to read these descriptions, but it is certainly another to see the pictures. This child was beautiful. She was full of life. Maria had a purpose in life and the end of it cannot be summed up as a tragedy because that is not strong enough a word to describe this traumatizing sequence of events. A Prosecuting Attorney from the area, said, "The desire for the drug perverts everything that is good in people."

Yet if using methamphetamine turns you into an unhealthy, child abusing pervert, then why do so many people use it? One meth user stated, "It's like a calm, inviting ocean on hot summer day. Diving into the drug feels so good. It's easy not to notice it's pull, pulling you out to sea…until your thirty miles out and too weak to fight it's pull. It feels like a million bucks." How does it feel *so* good?

Meth - also known as crank, dope, crystal, speed, go, and tweak as well as 348 other terms feels the way it does due to two neurotransmitters, or "pleasure juices," known as 'serotonin' and 'dopamine'. These chemicals are designed to be released during pivotal moments in life, such as when you get your first kiss, passing your driver's test, having a great night with your friends, scoring the date you have been waiting for, buying your first new car, or getting married. Yet methamphetamine manipulates, disintegrates and dissolves these designations.

Meth is used several ways including smoking, swallowing and injecting. Look at your bare foot and spread your toes. Users needle themselves in between their toes, so they can prevent other people from knowing. That is just the beginning of the length they will go in order to hide their use.

As meth enters the blood stream large amounts of serotonin and dopamine are released. The neurotransmitters are then accepted by the receptors in the brain, making it possible to experience heightened energy, euphoria (excessive happiness and feelings of well being), a decrease in the bodies need to eat and sleep, an increase of fight or flight instincts, and a super-charged sex drive. Feeling like a million bucks sounds pretty close. Overall, methamphetamine provides the user with *the illusion of reward without actually achieving anything,* and that, creates a *false sense of self worth.*

When the large amounts of these neurotransmitters are released, as caused by the drug, it permanently damages the receptor in the brain for two reasons. Firstly, the brain is not designed to hold large amounts of those chemicals at once and so it permanently destroys the receptors. Secondly, when the brain releases so many chemicals at one time, the brain immediately begins to alter itself in expectation to receive those chemicals in the same amount again. Therefore, the brain eliminates several receptors to avoid over load in the future. By doing this, however, means a user begins living a life without much feeling because so many chemicals have to be released to feel anything at all. Instinctually, a user tends to continue using to feel good because they have difficulty achieving a positive mental state on their own. Naturally, the more a person uses meth, the more damage it causes.

My science teacher, Mrs. Glass, played a very important role in my education. She stated that the body could only recycle 25% of all the serotonin and dopamine chemicals released. Those who are using frequently, as most meth users do, only 6.25% is recycled after a second use. If the user engages again it decreases to 1.56%. All the while the user trying to achieve what they had that ever first time, an impossible feat. You can wait long periods of time for the neurotransmitters to regain their effect but it will never be the same as the initial high.

The negative effects of methamphetamine highly outweigh the positive effects. Methamphetamine makes people paranoid. These people entertain an honest belief that someone is out to get them, be it the police or some crankster next door trying to rip off their dope, and it quickly turns quite dangerous. They set up hidden traps around their residence, stock up as many weapons as they possibly can, and plan battle strategies. They duct tape daggers under tables and desks, hide axes behind the television, and place guns in between couch cushions throughout the house. A small meth raid could turn up as many as forty to sixty weapons. Memories of surveillance footage relaying the recovery of such weapons makes my skin crawl. Not only are cranksters paranoid, but can be cold hearted violent, individuals as well.

Meth makes people extremely violent. I once knew a speed freak named Lori. She would spontaneously engage in violent activity. She pulled the banister out of the wall when a family member unexpectedly came to visit. She threatened to kill me, punched her boyfriend regularly, threw bricks through the window and broke the door knob off. She would steal cars and disappear for weeks, then come home and sleep for a month. She stole anything she could get her hands on and would pawn it off for drugs. It was a shame to watch this woman, who was originally a role model for me, turn into nothing. She went through the police academy and was an excellent cook, talented at crafts, and loved animals. Unfortunately the end product of her life revolved around tweaking and loosing all of those characteristics which had made her such a wonderful person. Last I heard, she was jobless, friendless, her family had disowned her, her animals were dead, and she was desperate.

Meth makes people depressed, as a result of the neurotransmitters exhausted in the process of using meth. It is difficult to find joy in anything when there are no chemicals left to feel simple happiness. Just as Lori would come home and sleep for long periods of time, there were no showers or chores accomplished. She would get up to eat and urinate and that was the extent of her daily activities. It is a hazardous lifestyle which prohibits any full accomplishment of anything. So the paranoid, cold-hearted, violent tweaks are dirty too.

Meth users age prematurely. A 40-year old tweaker looks like a 65-year old unhealthy individual. Kids who use meth develop haggard and pitiful looking personas and feel achy. Rather than turning back the clock, they hit fast forward every time they shoot up, smoke, or snort. It is easy to notice a long term user because they always have the nastiest teeth I have ever seen. Meth eats the enamel off of their teeth, which induces rot and dislodges them from the mandible.

Several videos are available on the lives of meth and cocaine involved families. One in particular displayed a bitter yet emotional reunion between two drug addicts after being released from jail and they engaged in a wet and sloppy open mouth kiss. There had to be a grand total of seven teeth between the two of them. Tooth loss can be hideous. I personally have dealt with several people who did not care for their teeth and used tons of drugs. It results in fake teeth, abscesses, infections and a whole host a problems associated with getting those last few teeth yanked. The tooth decay can even be passed onto their children.

Meth users tend to bald faster than everyone else. The hair really suffers. Users consistently report clumps of hair routinely fall out and are left all over the home. They deal with the shower drain constantly clogging up and to make matters worse, the hair that actually grows back is damaged, dry, and unhealthy. Therefore, the paranoid, cold-hearted, violent, dirty tweaks tend to be ugly too.

Abscesses do not solely occur in a user's mouth with the teeth aspect. Intravenous drugs are those put into the body via the needle. In cases where people are not thinking clearly, unclean needles are used frequently, or shared. In addition to HIV and other hideous diseases which can be transmitted, abscesses can occur also. An abscess occurs when the tissues being penetrated get infected and begin to disintegrate. The abscess becomes a gaping hole surrounded by inflammation and collects large amounts of pus. It is absolutely disgusting. A realistic, yet dark view on these effects, can be viewed in the movie *Requiem of a Dream*. It is a fabulous depiction of the truthful yet terrorizing reality of meth use. These disgusting infections can be cured, but left unattended results in amputation

Meth users totally stink. By stinking, I am referring to the chemical smell that literally permeates their surrounding. One meth user who is now in rehab recalled having to take several showers per day in order to minimize the stench of rot and chemicals oozing from his pores. Additionally, users suffer from bitter bones as they are robbed by the loss of adequate nutrition such as a healthy, balanced diet and rest. Broken bones and fractures are common among tweakers.

Meth eats a users internal organs. No kidding. Especially the brain - if you haven't noticed, most tweakers are socially incompetent. They speak way to fast, are jumpy, and constantly interrupt because they lack the self discipline to listen or be patient. They speak loudly and without pausing, jumping back and forth between three or four different subjects at any given time. This makes it almost unbearable to be near them for a long period of time. Often times the neurotransmitter receptors that induce the effects of the serotonin and dopamine are damaged and sometimes destroyed. Meth use contributes to hundreds of cases of severe kidney and heart damage, a risk none of us can afford. It may be fair to say that these paranoid, cold-hearted, violent, dirty, ugly, stinky, broken boney, abscessing, infected, balding, organ sacrificing cranksters don't have much going for them.

How does meth really hurt so horribly and change a person so much? Although new manufacturing formulas are constantly being developed, the potent chemicals needed for its manufacture are astonishing:

* Red Devil Lye - Rat poison

* Freon - Fluid used for air conditioners.

* Acetone - Nail polish remover

* Psuedoephedrine - Common in household cold medicines

* Iodine - Treats hoof rot in livestock

* Red Phosphorus - The red tip at the end of a match

* Anhydrous Ammonia - Used for farming purposes while held in hardcore canisters- when it gets on your skin it burns at a negative three hundred (-300) degrees. It'll burn you to the bone.

Can you imagine eating a combination burrito with those kinds of ingredients? Blah! Not to mention flammable! It is easy to understand why one (1) out of every six (6) meth labs explode. There are tons of toxic acids present, making meth labs extremely dangerous to children. These children have more developmental problems, are more likely to be sexually abused, tend to be more violent, have increased occurrences of lice infestation, as well as rotten teeth, according to the Seattle Times. Peace Officers and Children Service Workers constantly see these children encountering high levels of domestic abuse, pornography, junk food, weapons, hidden traps, and drug paraphernalia if their parents use meth. They tend to be behind in school, are malnourished, and do not respect boundaries.

Now when I mention that one (1) of every six (6) meth labs explode please understand many children are present at these scenes. Many fall injured or even die. I have seen children with portions of the face blown off and their bodies scarred and charred from the fire. These kids will never have a normal life. They will never be treated as a regular member of society and will have huge health problems and risks for the remainder of their life. A new effort to combat this are Drug Endangered Children Tasks Forces combining the efforts of District Attorney Investigators, Child Protective Services, Probation Officers, Sheriff Deputies, Police Officers, Social Workers, Nurses, and Counselors. They have a very difficult job and do this country a great service with their collaborative resources. Not all of these children are injured in explosions, however.

Recently a 16-year old mother fell asleep with her baby on the living room floor while manufacturing meth in a bucket in the kitchen. The baby woke up and crawled into the kitchen while mom was still out cold. Anyone familiar with children know that babies love to play with pans and buckets and such. This youngster was no different and the baby wound up falling into to bucket of chemicals. Immediately the baby began screaming and his mother came stumbling in. She picked up the baby and wrapped him in a towel, took him back into the living room, laid him on the couch, and went back to sleep. Several hours later, she woke up and saw that her baby's lips were blue, his tongue was white and he was having extreme difficulty breathing. She took him to the emergency room and learned the concoction had scarred the baby's lungs, and he would have medical problems for the rest of his life. He will never have the ability to reach his full potential because it was hindered by his own mother's poor choices. These poor choices have effects on children and society in general as it works its way to the government level.

Being that budget issues come up in any state, it is important to understand how expensive these meth labs are to clean up. Each meth lab costs between $3,000 and $150,000 to clean up depending on it's size and the State forks out the bill meaning tax payers of the State are paying for it! California has over 2,000 meth labs found per year. This creates a bill a minimum of $6 million and up to $300 million just for the purpose of cleaning labs. Certainly that money can be put to better use.

Glancing back to the few chemicals I listed, you can imagine the harm those chemicals might cause to water systems, soil, and other necessities of the environment. You probably noticed how harmful this is when considering our food, our water systems, even our air. Additionally, consider that every one (1) pound of methamphetamine produced creates five (5) to seven (7) pounds of toxic waste. This waste *does* pollute water supplies, and being that labs smell so bad the larger ones tend to be in rural farming areas. Additionally, exploding labs have contributed in the creation of devastating forest fires.

Methamphetamine is a terrible plague which is perverting everything good in people, and in life. Methamphetamine is terrifying.

CHAPTER 5 - FAMOUS ECSTASY

Have you ever heard of MDMA? X? XTC? Adam? Rolls? The Love or Hug Drug? Obviously we know that substance is Ecstasy. Truthfully, there are several desired effect which teenagers and young adults find extremely appealing such as pleasure, self satisfaction, the lights shine brighter, music sounds sweeter, touch is hyper sensitive and sensual, the user develops a strong sense of community, they love everyone and forgiveness of all enemies. Overall, ecstasy provides its user with the illusions that all is right with the world.

Unfortunately, all of these effects are a fallacy. I will never forget when I first began researching drugs. I had two roommates who would attend Raves and experiment with ecstasy. I was cooking dinner one night and one of the two came in to socialize. I told her how I had become fascinated with the manufacturing of drugs and how awful they were really turning out to be. I continued to tell her about how I planned to research Ecstasy next and confessed I knew she had been using it. So I asked her one simple question.

"What is in ecstasy?"

"Oh it's great! It's this little pill and it makes you feel sooo good!" She happily replied.

"I know what it is, what I want to know is what is *in* it."

"It's just 100% Ecstasy."

"No, that isn't right, Ecstasy is not even really called Ecstasy, it's MDMA."

"No Jess, you don't even know what you're talking about it is just total Ecstasy and it makes you feel so good."

At the time I thought I may have been misinformed but I did not think you could boil a bunch of roots together and get Ecstasy. It was at that time I realized no one has any freaking idea what this stuff is. Please allow me to set the record straight.

Ecstasy is called MDMA, which is 3,4 methylenedioxymet hamphetamine. If you will kindly read the word again, you may notice the word methamphetamine in that long crazy combination of letters. That's right, in real Ecstasy, which can be difficult to find, a large portion of that little pill is methamphetamine. So what is methylenedioxy?

Ecstasy is a combination of methamphetamine and mescaline (methylenedioxy). Mescaline is a derivative of the peyote cactus. When this cactus is ingested, it causes the one who ate it to become nauseous and throw up. After vomiting it allows the user to hallucinate. This is the element that provides an ecstasy user with the hallucinogen effects.

So Ecstasy, in addition to the effects of methamphetamine (paranoia, violence, depression, premature aging, tooth rot, brain damage, kidney damage, heart damage and hair loss in chunks), there are an entire new variety of consequences be it the methamphetamine is combined with the mescaline. The most prevalent is probably dehydration, I am talking 106-107-108- even 109 degrees Fahrenheit! Talk about brain boil! That happens as the body cannot sweat while under the influence of Ecstasy, therefore, without the proper hydration with water, the body temperature rises in the high energy environments Ecstasy use is prevalent.

There has been another risk revealed, however, in regard to this concept. Now Ecstasy users have been dying not only from the high temperatures but also from drinking too much water. I remember when I was a kid I heard on the news about a girl who had been in trouble and her father made her drink 16 glasses of water as a punishment. She died, and it makes sense why. The body can only hold so much water, so Ecstasy users have been consuming tons and tons of water, only to wind up dead from trying to prevent death by high temperatures. Interesting, yet sad. There has been many warnings encouraging users to drink plenty of water, but very rarely do they know not to drink to much of it.

Ecstasy users experience the effects for six to twelve hours. Teens have told me that they feel left out not going to Raves because their friends, are so excited on Friday, and all they talk about the following week is how much fun they had at the Rave. What their friends don't tell them, is that they felt like they had been hit by a car the next day. While I was public speaking on one occasion, a member of the audience volunteered to announce he had consumed three ecstasy pills and went home, slept for two hours and went to work. He said that it did not make you feel bad the next day. I asked the young man if he had ever used Ecstasy before that date. He said no. I asked him if he had bought all three pills from the same person. He said yes. I proceeded to inform him he had been ripped off and what he had consumed was not Ecstasy but someone probably peddling sugar pills with caffeine in them. One of the best ways I have remained informed of what types of Ecstasy contains what type of chemicals, is the following website: www.dancesafe. com. It is a controversial group, who tests the Ecstasy pills at Raves to prevent the possibility of a fatality. Some people believe it is encouraging youth to use drugs, and then again, they also provide the users with tons of current information on the risks of ecstasy. Therefore it can go either way.

While under the influence of Ecstasy, the user frequently experiences jaw lock. Jaw lock is when the muscles of the jaw tighten and spasm uncontrollably. Some kids have actually involuntarily bit their own tongue off. As a result, objects have been found to allow users to cater to the effects. For example, you will rarely find an Ecstasy user without a pacifier, ring pop, tootsie roll pop, or tongue stud. Anything that keeps the jaw moving tends to keep it from biting the tongue off.

Even if someone uses Ecstasy one single time, brain damage results, not only to the neurotransmitter (pleasure juice) receptors but also to areas of the brain critical to thought and memory. There are many monkeys to thank for their involvement in the tests necessary to have established that fact. That has become a well known fact as it has been broadcasted on several popular television talk shows and programs.

Prolonged Ecstasy use can create an acne-like rash. If you ever run into someone with this symptom or have it yourself, it is very important ecstasy use is terminated completely. It is a symptom signifying severe liver damage.

Ecstasy use can make a teenager appear as though they have Parkinson's Disease when they drive. Parkinson's Disease occurs when muscles begin to detach from the bone, leading to involuntary shaking and the inability to control certain muscle movements. Sometimes the user will suffer from irreversible altered motor skills due to the excessive brain damage.

So, now for the final effect and consequence which proves to be rather controversial. Is Ecstasy addictive...some say yes and some say no. Although I have never used Ecstasy myself and though my roommates always said they didn't have to use it but chose to...the fact that they continued to go back to it even after I moved from there, and the fact that the real stuff contains methamphetamine, a substance that makes people do things they normally wouldn't do with a gun to their head, makes me tend to agree with the philosophy that it is addictive. Meth is so dangerously addictive as discussed in the previous chapter. Wouldn't Maria's aunt and uncle have stopped shooting meth before they boiled her to death if they could? So now I am asking you, how can Ecstasy *not* be addictive if much of authentic Ecstasy is methamphetamine?

Ecstasy is a danger to every teenager. Why is it a threat to you, even if you do not use it? Nine of every ten teenagers have a clothing item of some sort which has a butterfly, smiley face, superman emblem, Pikachu depiction, blue dolphins or Tasmanian devils. What do these trends have to do with illegal drugs? The imprints on the Ecstasy tablets are butterflies and cartoons and business logos and any animal that becomes popular. Teens can identify with these pills, and call it their own as a means of establishing their identity at the Raves. For example, Sandra uses "Dancer," because she's a darn good dancer. Stephen takes "Euro" because he went to Europe last summer so he identifies with that. Molly rolls with "Tweety" because she has a Tweety fetish, Dan hunts for "Cookies and Cream" because that is his favorite, Jamie is all about "Butterfly" because she wants to fly. That is what I am talking about. Ecstasy is probably the most dangerous drug out there, not solely because of it's effect but also due to the promoters attaching Ecstasy to the epitome of teenage culture.

CHAPTER 6 - ECSTASY'S RIGHT HAND DRUG

When you read the word *Everclear* what do you think of? Most people think of a band, but it is also known as ecstasy's right hand drug. Liquid X, G, Grievous Bodily Harm, Great Hormones at Bedtime, Scoop, and Everclear, most popularly known as GHB, is officially GammaHydroxyButerate.

GHB can kill you, it is responsible for more than 70 deaths in the last year and dozens more are being investigated by the Drug Enforcement Administration. It is more potent than anyone can appreciate. If you have a bottle of water nearby, go grab it. Unscrew the cap, turn it upside down and look at it. That is a measured shot of GHB- it will inebriate you quickly, as that shot is the equivalent to ten glasses of wine. Most people would not be able to handle that.

Not too long ago a girl in college who stood in the middle of a group of friends and bought an actual shot glass full of GHB, approximately three shots of GHB - the dealer at the party figured she would take a small sip and pass it around to her friends. The girl downed the whole thing. The dealer's jaw dropped. He mouthed, "You just committed suicide- I'm out of here." Immediately blood started pouring from her nose and her mouth, a sign of pulmonary edema (left heart valve failure). Her sister grabbed her and carried her out to her car. They rushed to the hospital, only five miles away. There is no cure for a GHB overdose, you can't even throw it up because GHB paralyzes your gagging reflexes, so her sister watched in horror as the 20 year old beauty fell into a coma. Eventually, her family was forced to pull the plug.

How can GHB be so potent? Well first off, GHB is generally manufactured in bathtubs, at least the stuff you encounter at parties is. Yes… bathtubs. I used to have a pot bellied pig and I bathed him in my bathtub. People do really strange and unsual things in bathtubs. They are gross, collecting that oily line of filth along the lower portion of the tub, or picking out the black stuff that jams in the corners of toenails…people do really gross things in bathtubs.

So Mr. GHB Maker throws engine degreaser and floor stripper along with a dozen other ingredients and Boom - there's GHB. It is a yellowish, transparent liquid that is a little soapy, and slightly salty but can pass for water. So not only does is strip your insides but it contributes to memory loss.

GHB is the number one date rape drug in the United States. You may recall a rape counselor from San Diego, California. She went to a small party consisting of one close girlfriend and two male acquaintances. One of them spiked her margarita with GHB and she became immediately intoxicated. One of her gentleman acquaintances escorted her off into a bedroom where she passed out. She awoke to find the man raping her. When he realized she was awake, he began beating her face to the point of unconsciousness. She has been traumatized since. That woman who assisted in helping the lives of dozens of people, will never be the same.

GHB is easy to disguise because it has no odor, and unfortunately, due to it's immediate effects and lack of education concerning the drug, people tend to use recklessly. I used to know a young lady in college named Sadie. She went to a nearby dance club under the influence of GHB. While she was dancing, she became sick so she ran to the bathroom. After vomiting all over herself and the restroom stall, she passed out. Her friends figured she had left with the guy she had been dancing with so they left her there. Sadie was not found until security was doing it's final checks long after last call. It took her forever to get home, it was a bad situation. I sure wish Sadie had taken basic steps to avoid such a predicament - like not use GHB.

I have developed a list of tips to minimize your chances of being drugged. As mentioned before, I am in no way condoning alcohol use. It's irresponsible use is defiling and turns even the most respectable individuals into crawling, violent, sniveling animals who cannot think straight. However, safety comes first. Please take notice to these tips and employ them always.

1) Don't drink alcohol until you are the legal age of 21 in the United States.

2) BYOB (Bring Your Own Beverage) - Try to bring beverages which have a replaceable lid.

3) Pour your own drink at all times.

4) Do not try mystery concoctions.

5) Do not try energy drinks made at parties.

6) Stay away from beverages which would easily conceal the slightly salty taste such as Margaritas, Long Island Ice Teas, or Goldshlager.

7) Cover your drink at all times, get in the habit of carrying drinks with your hand over the top.

8) Never leave sight of the people in the room.

9) Use the buddy system, if you notice anyone gone, go find them.

10) Keep in mind there is more than GHB that can be slipped into your drink, respond accordingly.

In addition, please know that this is not just a chapter for the ladies reading, but for the gentlemen as well. If you attend a party and notice a friend acting completely drunk when they have had two or three sips of their drink, keep your eye on them because predators are tough to pick out of a crowd.

CHAPTER 7 - ANTI-CEREAL SPECIAL K

Ketamine Hydrochloride is also known as Super K, Vitamin K, Gas, Blast and especially, Special K. You do not add milk to it and it is not eaten with a spoon. This drug is extremely addictive. Many times when I ask a crowd what this is, it is most popularly known as a cat anesthetic. That is wrong, however, if it were only a cat or dog anesthetic, perhaps it would not be so harmful, but unfortunately it subdues horses and elephants in preparation for surgery. This is strong stuff.

I tend to call ketamine users the Dissociative Phenomena Club. Members of this club experience relaxation and heightened sexual experiences because everything is magnified. They mentally leave their body and go elsewhere - agitated and estranged, they commonly become delirious. Special K puts users in a dream-like state... unable to tell what is real and what is a figment of their imagination.

True crime author, Ann Rule, wrote a section about a yoga master, Marcia Moore, in *A Rage To Kill*, who became involved with using ketamine hydrochloride as a means of pursuing her past lives and meditating to bring greater wellness and peace for the next life. Prior to using ketamine, she was extremely respected, and brilliant in many ways. Her close friends were happy for her when she married a man who was crazy about her. He was a doctor and obtained permission to do research on ketamine. They began experimenting with ketamine hydrochloride in sessions. He stopped participating as he never became comfortable with the feeling of parting with the body, whereas Marcia loved it and finally felt complete with it. She grew further and further away from her friends and family until one day she simply disappeared. Most believe she went off under it's influence and it eventually led to her destruction.

"A man [or woman] who strays from the path of understanding comes to rest in the company of the dead." Proverbs 21:16

Being under the influence in crowded places is particularly dangerous. One of the instant dangers is that a user can become totally helpless as they are in a "dissociative reality," where the things that they see are half dreams. Imagine yourself at a concert with a friend who is under the influence of Special K. You friend sees a dragon fly over your head, scream and gets on the ground. You, being a good friend, lean over and tell them everything is okay but they don't know if you are real or fake and you might be in with the dragon so they freak out even more. I have read and heard countless stories involving this sort of behavior. An interesting note, is the fact that ketamine hydrochloride is it's chemically related to PCP.

CHAPTER 8 - THE LIVING NIGHTMARE: PCP

We have all heard of PCP, Killer Weed, Angel Dust, Rocket Fuel - Phencyclidine. PCP leads people to experience terrifying hallucinations, unconsciousness, invincibility, the inability to feel pain, lack of fear, and possibly death.

When I worked at Juvenile Hall, I had a resident approach me to tell me about his home pass (a weekend at home). He said, *"I got to see my girlfriend this weekend, but we are not together anymore."* I asked him what happened and he shook his head. *"She brought some pot over as a welcome home for the weekend present, and that was cool. I knew Mama would kill us, you know, so we climbed on top of a two story building to smoke it. Then she pulled out this stuff I'd never seen and I asked her what it was. She told me it was angel dust and she sprinkled it onto her joint then offered me some. I told the woman, 'I wanna see what it does to you, then maybe I'll try it.' She put it away and we smoked our joints and I was just chillin' and lookin' at the sky when she jumped up and told me she could fly. I told her I knew she was my pigeon and all but to sit back down. She told me she wanted to show me, that she was going to take off the side of the building! I told her Red Bull gives you wings, not weed or angel dust, but she just laughed and leaped off the side of the building. I jumped over to the edge of the roof and saw her laying on the ground. I called to her to make sure she was alright and she jumped up and started laughing hysterically and ran off, leaving me on the roof."*

"So you broke up with her because she left you on the roof?" I asked, wondering if there was anything left. He proceeded the tell me his girlfriend eventually wound up at home and passed out. The next morning, her mother followed groaning noises coming from the bedroom. Upon viewing her daughter's appearance, the woman screamed and rushed her to the emergency room. Medical personnel took a multitude of X-rays and discovered every bone in her face had been shattered. *"And that's why I dumped her, for being so stupid."* All from adding a little angel dust to her Mary Jane, she lost her Juvenile Hall Prince Charming.

People who use PCP are never the same again. In regard to this drug, the whole community comes together against the police when a user needs to be arrested and winds up dead. Yet what the community doesn't see is the footage of people under the influence of PCP who threaten officer safety because any means used by officers to get the suspect into custody is then used against the officers. There is a mechanism similar to a paintball gun that has wire with hooks on it called a tazer. I have seen this used on a man under the influence of PCP. The wire wrapped around him and the hooks penetrated the skin. The subject ripped the hooks out of his flesh, unwound the wire and started swinging it above his head, flinging it at the officers. Unbelievable, don't you think? When these folks have weapons, they are deadly, and may be shot in order to protect the safety of officers and civilians alike. People always wonder why police officers don't just shoot them in the leg instead of the chest, where it will probably kill them. Officers are training to only pull their guns if they intend to kill. If the subject is shot in the leg, they can still do harm to the officers.

What makes PCP users so dangerous? When a person who has evil intentions is adrenalized to the maximum point, they can easily take on five people and win. When that same person cannot feel pain and will not follow instructions because they believe it is a dream - they cannot decipher what is real. Therefore, that person becomes a gigantic risk to everyone around - they hurt, they injure, and they kill.

One individual was once subdued and tranquilized. The suspect was booked into jail and placed in a padded room with a single door with a covered window which could be slid away for someone to observe the inside of the room. The man had been handcuffed to the wall, and a nurse went to check on him to see if he was stirring as the tranquilizer wore off. The nurse slid the cover from the window and the man was staring at her directly on the other side of the door. He had pulled his hands out of his handcuffs by ripping the skin and flesh off of his hands and breaking his bones to slide them out. He could not feel the intense pain, because he thought he was dreaming when he did it. When the effects wore off, and the pain kicked in, he was singing a different song.

CHAPTER 9 - WHACKED OUT LSD

Even the name sounds scary - Lysergic Acid Diethylamide, also known as Trips, Blotter, Doses and most popularly Acid. LSD is the most potent hallucinogenic drug known to man. It is important to know that it is readily available in most large communities. Here is an activity to demonstrate the potency of LSD:

Get a penny.

Hold it in one hand and think about how much that penny weighs.

Hold out your other hand and try to guess how many hits would of LSD would be present if that same weight was LSD. I have rarely heard a student or parent guess more than 500. Most guess between 10 and 100. What is your guess?

Some have guessed ten thousand hits are present in the weight equivalent to that of a penny. The truthful answer is fifty-six thousand hits. Can you picture someone dividing that penny over 56,000 blotter papers, microdots, stickers, temporary tattoos, window panes (jello squares) and sugar cubes? Extremely challenging, particularly without high tech equipment or half a lifetime of experience. Of course the average LSD manufacturer has neither. Why is that so dangerous? Extra hit means extra fun right? Not exactly because the extra hit can really pack a punch when it comes to eliminating one's sanity.

The lives of people who have used too much LSD sound more like nightmares than reality. In actuality, LSD creates a living nightmare. Kevin, for example, became an orange and stayed that way. He is currently being housed in a mental institution but the guy literally believes he is an orange. He sits with his arms wrapped around his body and runs from everyone in fear they will move his arms. In Kevin's mind, if someone moves his arms they are peeling him he will die. From what experts can tell, he will remain this way for the rest of his life.

Then there is Sharon. Sharon is a puddle, if anyone comes near her she screams bloody murder because if she is stepped on, she believes will die. As a puddle, she is living in the midst of permanent chaos of an LSD ruined life. True stories, real people, poor choices that led to throwing their life away. So much waste for nothing.

Furthermore, it is my understanding LSD stores in the tail bone, giving way to back flashes and such. I have never actually seen proof of this, but several drug users maintain they have had spinal taps checking their LSD level to see if that is what is making them go insane. Most people would not appreciate a long needle penetrating their back bone.

It takes approximately fifteen minutes to feel the effects of LSD set in- the sweating, nausea, dilating pupils, and gooseflesh. Under the influence of LSD there is no control and the user experiences a complete immediate separation between body and reality. When your mind takes a turn for the worst and you imagine something bad happening, you cannot stop it. That is called a "Bad Trip." What does a bad trip look like? A big gorilla comes barging through the front door with a machine gun shooting notes going along with whatever you are listening to. You start dodging behind chair and tables and your stuck in this scenario - this illusion - for ten to twelve hours.

If you and I were to be sitting in a room and an oak tree with a juke box slammed through the window on one side and a cobra snake with a gold tooth slithered out the of the television screen, we could see the music from the juke box and hear the colors all around us. The next day, we would experience the aftermath of using LSD, fighting severe depression for a long time, suffering severe anxiety, and we possibly experiencing terrifying flash backs.

CHAPTER 10 - HUFFSTER

Overall, the most popular huffing material at the present time is nitrous oxide. Most people are familiar with this stuff and if you are not, you should be. It takes a group of very desperate people to get high of off whip cream canisters, but that doesn't stop them. It is the gas that makes the cream shoot out. It is laughing gas. Teens actually inhale it to get high. This is extremely dangerous because the human body is not designed to handle the poisonous fumes. Dentists have licenses to use it in accompaniment of their practice to aid their patients in time of surgery. Nitrous Oxide and other chemicals found in cleaning or painting products are not intended for recreational use.

If you go to www.resort.com/~banshee/Info/N2O/nitrous.dangers/html you will find the following information:

&* Nitrous Oxide leads to Oxygen Deprivation, in which case hypoxia occurs. Hypoxia is a condition in which tissues are starved of oxygen. If the hypoxia is not reversed quickly, body tissue begins to die.

- Frost Bite - When nitrous oxide is inhaled directly from the tanks, the gas is extremely cold and can cause frost bite on your lips, mouth and nose.

- Loss of Motor Control - Under the influence of nitrous oxide, the user usually reels around and falls to the ground. That is why dentists and oral surgeons always require a designated driver when using it. Motor control is completely out of the question.

- Vitamin B-12 Interference - Vitamin B-12 is crucial for a healthy body, using nitrous oxide prohibits the body from accepting B-12 as a nutrient and therefore bone marrow and nervous system damage are possiblities.

- Folic Acid Interference - Folic Acid contributes to red blood cell production. Such production is hindered when Nitrous Oxide is inhaled into the body.

- Huffing blocks oxygen intake which causes nausea and motion sickness.

The following is the Never-Never List :

🔥 Never try to inhale N2O (nitrous oxide) directly from whippits or point escaping gas at anyone. The gas will give you frost burn.

🔥 Never strap a gas mask to your face because if you pass out, the one thing you will need is oxygen. People have died doing this.

🔥 Never lock yourself in a room, closet, car, or fridge with a tank of N2O and open it. People have died doing this.

🔥 Never huff standing up.

🔥 Never huff near open windows.

🔥 Never use a large tank without a regulator that has not been strapped down.

🔥 Never use homemade nitrous, you will have made toxic gases.

After inhaling any volatile chemicals, permanent brain damage can be caused limiting the possibilities to learn. There is much to lose and nothing to gain from huffing.

CHAPTER 11 - COCAINE DREAMS

In the 1970's ad 1980's, cocaine was a serious problem- it was the most frequently used stimulant. Cocaine comes from Bolivia, Columbia and Peru. It is manufactured and then trafficked into the United States, where it is converted to crack (a deadly and highly addictive form of cocaine), with common household items.

Cocaine is also known as blow, white, coke, snow, nose candy, or snort. It creates an incredible high which lasts between five and fifteen minutes. Remember reading about Methamphetamine? You may recall that when it is used, the neurotransmitters or "pleasure juices" known as serotonin and dopamine are released. When someone uses cocaine all of the happy juices are released at one time. Cocaine must feel incredible, but it is not worth it, because no additional use of cocaine will ever feel that good again. The entire pleasure supply is sacrificed as it is dispensed over the course of a few minutes. As you recall, only 25% of the serotonin and dopamine that are released can be recycled, and that is not enough to recycle the original high.

After the intense high, your body goes numb. In the movie *Blow,* starring Johnny Depp and Penelope Cruz, there was a scene where a man snorted cocaine he was planning to buy. After brief conversation, he humorously interrupts with, "I can't feel my face." That was because his body was in shock. Truthfully, cocaine use does not feel great the entire time - when an individual snorts cocaine, they make a funny face, and the reason for that is snorting cocaine feels like getting punched in the nose. Despite that fact, cocaine remains incredibly addictive.

The addictive factor of cocaine is the intense high. Users will continuously use cocaine over and over again in order to achieve the initial, amazing high. Of course, the pleasure juices are gone so achieving the same high again, is absolutely impossible.

How can anyone care about anything when they feel no joy? It is a harsh truth where humanly monsters are created. When you hear about new mothers leaving their crack babies at the hospital, abandoning their own flesh and blood, this is an effect of cocaine use. The cocaine eliminates maternal instincts in these cases, defying nature. It is difficult to see a crack baby and to learn what the drug has done to newborns. Often times these babies are born with serious birth defects, such as breathing problems and lifelong challenges. The lips of a crack baby has great difficulty grasping a bottle, therefore, they tend to grow weak do to their inability to feed. They suffer from low birth weight, nutrient deficiency, and when you kiss their cheeks, you can taste the chemicals on their skin. Infants exposed to cocaine require constant physical contact, and their bodies undergo such withdrawal turmoil they cry and are not able to be consoled. On a lighter note, if provided two healthy parents who make every effort to do right by the child in the area of child development, granting tremendous amounts of loving attention, the child can be "caught up," by age five. The initial destruction, however, can impact a child for their entire life - being that cocaine is so harmful. It is a wonder people continue to manufacture cocaine.

The most prevalent entity which drives the cocaine industry is money. Dealing drugs pulls in the bucks. Most drug dealers and traffickers do not hang around with their customers so rarely do they see the impact first-hand. They know things occur, but block out the poison they have brought to other's lives, in exchange for their drive for money. Those who run the cocaine industry and make it work do not care about other people. The people who use cocaine make them wealthy and other than that, those people are expendable. Cocaine pushers maintain a cold perspective while claiming they are just doing business.

A second reason the cocaine industry is maintained revolves around jobs. In the United States, there are a multitude of jobs and careers people can choose to pursue. Cultural anthropology courses teach that in the areas of Bolivia, Columbia and Peru cocaine is manufactured, jobs are not prevalent, there are only two choices. You can either be a prostitute or work for the cocaine company. Both are undesirable, and given the choice, which on would you choose?

No one wants to sell their body. Women tend to be successful in the prostitution circuit although it can be self destructive. Many women prostitutes in the United States tend to work in order to support their drug habits. Women prostitutes in Bolivia, Columbia, and Peru work to support their poverty famished families. These countries lack such luxuries as birth control options, therefore this line of work contributes to population growth. In turn, creating another mouth to feed and even greater poverty. Therefore, employment by the cocaine company creates a new field of options for these people, and possibly some hope as well.

Paco, an average Peruvian, goes to work for the cocaine company. Generally, the women pick the leaves for the manufacture process, and the best positions are reserved for relatives of the management, therefore Paco is assigned to manufacture. On his first day, Paco's supervisor shows him how to take the lids off bathtub-sized containers and pour the coca leaves into the tub that contains a substance with powerful fumes. Paco asks his supervisor what causes the fumes. The supervisor replies it is none of his business and informs him that if he asks again, he will be fired. Paco is forced to measure correct portions of intense liquids, not realizing it is kerosene and gasoline. He is responsible to soak the leaves, mix the concoction, and mash until it becomes the desired texture.

Soaking the leaves is simple, Paco pours in the leaves and the chemicals and allows it to sit for a long period of time. Mixing is a tricky, as the only instrument with the correct temperature and texture to get the most potent outcome is the human hand. Gloves are not acceptable. So Paco places his hand in the large containers and begins to mix as he directed. His hands beginning to itch, but ignores it because he knows he must mash next. So Paco stands in the tub and steps in place. After having his skin submerged in the gasoline for a short amount of time, he notices a slight burning sensation. Paco does not realize the concoction is eating his flesh. Despite the itching and stinging, Paco will not complain because does not want to be fired. He has heard rumors of other villagers being shot to death for knowing about the manufacture. So Paco presses on.

Paco soaks, mixes, and mashes several times and gradually begins to develop serious problems with his limbs. Constantly submitting is hands into the liquid eats the flesh off his fingers. Soon, he has only useless stumps in place of his hands. Paco can not quit his jobs because he has to support his family, and he knows they will starve without the sacrifice of his hands. Yet now that his hands are mere stumps, they are useless. So Paco learns how to manufacture with his feet. Before long, Paco can hardly walk. Paco is a victim of his home and must suffer to such an extent to make ends meet. Many people are subjected to Paco's fate as their birthplace and social class is such.

As cocaine is manufactured in these other countries, many people wonder how cocaine finds its way into the United States. Cocaine travels just like people do, by airplane, boat, or vehicle. Cocaine is easy to conceal and traffickers hide drugs I unusual compartments where a scent could be avoided by drug dogs. Those three countries supply the entire world with cocaine, and only a mere yet 10% of Columbia's cocaine efforts are administered to the United States. Twelve Semi trucks or three airplanes could make that happen. As you can imagine, it must be easy to smuggle the cocaine amongst the coffee beans and other products from the southern countries. People who are desperate to continue using know it is an expensive habit to maintain. It is worth it to the traffickers - since the pay off is so big.

One tiny little crack rock costs only $2.00, but it won't do you much good. A typical user will spend an average of $1,000.00 per week to support their habit. I know one woman who burned her $17,000.00 inheritance to maintain her drug addition. People will pay big money to avoid withdrawal. If they become totally broke and no longer can afford cocaine, many turn to methamphetamine use. The withdrawal symptoms of cocaine include: Involuntary teeth grinding, weight loss, face picking, paranoia, dizziness, tremors, agitation, panic, hostility, abdominal cramps, chest pain and palpitations. The withdrawal symptoms are a result of the body trying to re-learn how to function with the absence of the drug. Withdrawal may appear like a pitiful existence, yet is better than overdose.

If a user consumes too much cocaine within a short amount of tie, there is a high risk of cardiac arrest, strokes or death. Some cocaine users begin going thought withdrawal and cannot handle it and return to using. Sometimes they lose control and go on a cocaine binge. Many youth are curious about cocaine and therefore the trend is currently on the rise according to information provided to School Resource Officers.

CHAPTER 12 - BLACK HOLE HEROIN

Heroin is a derivative of opium, such as codeine and morphine. Becoming involved with heroin is far more dangerous than medical use of the latter two.

Exploring a hypothetical experience, imagine a buddy of yours approaches you when you are on your way home. He is someone you consider a friend, someone you respect. He begins to tell you about these eye drops that give you a rush, make you feel tired but awake - "You have got to try it!" he invites. Assuming you are fairly cautious about your physical safety you may ask, "What is it?" or "Where did you get it?" Your friend tells you, "I got them from my older brother. He told me it's heroin, but I don't think it is because you can only inject heroin."

The friend has made a common assumption heroin is always used intravenously. Heroin comes in many forms and can be injected, smoked, eaten, or snorted. Many new advertising techniques have been developed by drug pushers, such as spreading rumors, that reintroduce heroin. The goal is to convince young people to dismiss the picture of the old, socially inadequate, skinny heroin addict by replacing it with a synthetic heroin social user. By spreading the word synthetic heroin is more healthy and less harmful, looking more like China White than traditional Black Tar Heroin. Synthetic heroin in the eye drops contain microscopic crystals that destroy the blood vessels in the eyes. The damage causes a persons eyes to become permanent blood shot. Even though they appear to be simply eye drops, they remain as dangerous and as deadly.

When an individual begins to use heroin they must intake more and more of the drug to achieve the same high as before. The same high must be achieved or the body with go into withdrawal. Eventually, the dose will be so high the drug will over-ride the body and kill the user.

I know these two amazing teens, Sierra and Dean. Sierra is going to be a famous singing star one day and Dean has made a 360 degree turn from being headed down the wrong path to a model citizen. Their father was a heroin user and he received it cut with chlorine and powered milk. Most users don't know what their getting. Most users don't realize some substances don't dissolve in the blood stream - between the poison, the heroin dose, and the failure to dissolve, their father fell into a coma and had to be supported by machines in order to live. Those poor kids had to see their dad like that. Isn't that terrible? Of course, they are going to wind up positive because of a lot of changes they had to undergo, but that is something they never should have seen. That father abandoned his beautiful children for heroin, and that breaks my heart.

Often times, in the addicts mind, eventual overdose is easier to cope with than the withdrawal process. If you have ever seen the movie *Trainspotting*, you have an idea what this miserable time is like. It is painful, as the drug tries to purge itself from the body. I sat with a 16-year old teen throughout an entire night in juvenile hall while he went through withdrawal. He cried uncontrollably, hallucinating, and aching all over, the child sat huddled in a corner, bleeding from his nose and mouth, hacking up nasty mysterious phlegm and trying to make reasonable efforts to accept the fact he was HIV positive. It was almost unbearable for this minor and one of the most challenging experiences I ever had to endure. I never wish heroin withdrawal on anyone, or it's use. Heroin sucks its victims in like a black hole, before long, the user does not even have a choice, they become a slave to the drug. Every heroin user I have ever known has died, including that young man.

The effects that can be induced during the use of heroin includes spontaneous abortion, collapsed veins, infectious diseases such as infections of the heart lining and valves, abscesses, cellulites, liver disease, and respiratory depression. Amazing is that forty percent of high school seniors do not believe there is a great risk in trying heroin according to The Anti-Drug website. As demonstrated through the lives of Sierra and Dean, the wrath of heroin rains on the just and the unjust. It has no biases or preferences. Yet we can contain it and trap it, because we control the demand for the drug. That is our power against it.

Treatment options are available, methadone treatments can wean a user from heroin use. The benefit of methadone is that it subtracts the most intense withdrawal symptoms from the picture. When things get hard in this struggle, as we try to lead people away from the use of heroin, many turn to God, for support, for strategy, and for the courage to return to the life they knew before drugs.

EPILOGUE

I pray this book has aided you in many ways. This is not a time to grieve but a time to rejoice as we are taking the first steps to end this fitful grip on our community. Generations before have failed, yet this generation has more heart, strength, and inspiration than any before. On a personal note, I want you to know how precious your life is, how important you are to be alive in the world today. Your face is a part of the future, and which part you will play is up to you. At this point in time you have the ability to choose who you are, what kind of a life you will live, and why. Will you sit back and watch the world pass you by, or do you want more? Ultimately it is up to you, but keep in mind that using controlled substances and alcoholic beverages will provide large obstacles by potentially crashing your future. The goal in life is to reach your full potential. A life without drugs can secure our ability to achieve such accomplishments in your life.

We have little control over the supply of drugs. They will always be available in society. The power we do have, is in the demand for the drug. With a choice you make to avoid participating in its use.

For some people to grasp the reality of drug use and addiction, it takes witnessing a sister dying in your arms or a young man going through withdrawal where nothing can cease his pain and agony. Others, however, have enough wisdom, courage, and self respect to play offense rather than defense, and in turn, achieve their full potential. This is accomplished by committing to excellence. I wish the best upon your future, and whole heartedly appreciate the time you have spent to learn about these issues.

References

George Andrews and David Solomon, Editors, *The Coca Leaf and Cocaine Papers* (New York: Harcourt Brace Jovanovich, 1975).

Lester Greenspoon and James B. Bakalar, *Cocaine: a Drug and It's Social Evolution* (New York: Basic Books, 1976).

S.J. Mule, Editor in Chief, *Cocaine: Chemical, Biological, Clinical, Social, and Treatment Aspects* (Cleveland: CRC Press, 1976).

Paul Eddy, Hugo Sabogal, and Sara Walden, *The Cocaine Wars* (New York: Norton, 1988).

Leslie E. Moser, *Crack, Cocaine, Methamphetamine, and Ice* (Waco, Texas: Multi-Media Productions, 1980).

Mitch Earleywine, *Understanding Marijuana: A New Look At The Scientific Evidence* (Oxford, New York: Oxford University Press, 2002).

Nick Brownley, *The Complete Illustrated Guide to Cannabis* (London Sactuary 2003)

The Active Health Report on Alcohol, Tobacco, and Marijuana (Canada: Health and Welfare, 1989).

David Gene Peck, *Belief, Deterence, and Marjuana Use* (Saratoga, CA: Century Twenty One, 1980).

Video: Produced and Directed by: Paul J. Steibreoner, *Marijuana: The Mirror That Magnifies* (Ashland, Oregon: Haight-Ashbury Drug Clinic and CNS Productions, Inc., 1996).

Bruce Eisner, *Ecstacy: The MDMA Story* (Berkeley, CA: Ronin Pulishing, Inc., 1989).

Richard Hammersly, Furzana Khan, and Jason Ditton, *Ecstasy And The Rise Of The Chemical Generation* (London, New York: Routledge, 2002).

Julie Holland, Editor, *Ecstasy: The Complete Guide: A Comprehensive Look at the Risks and Benefits of MDMA* (Rochester, VA: Park Stret Press, 2001).

Richard Cohen, *The Love Drug: Marching to the Beat of Ecstasy* (New York: Haworth Medical Press, 1998).

Jerome Beck and Marsha Rosenbaum, *The Pursuit of Ecstasy: The MDMA Experience* (Albany: State University of New York Press, 1994).

Martin H. Lee and Bruce Shlain, *Acid Dreams: Complete Social History of LSD/ The CIA, The Sixties, and Beyond* (New York: Grove Weidenfeld, 1992).

Sidney Cohen, *Beyond Within: The LSD Story* (New York: Atheneum, 1967).

Allen Geller and Maxwell Boas, *The Drug Beat* (New York: Cowles Book Co., 1969).

D.V. Siva. Sankar, *LSD: A Total Story* (Westbury New York: PJD Publications, 1975).

Roberto Cavanna and Emilio Servadio, *ESP Experiments With LSD 25 and Psilocybin; A Medical Approach* (New York: Parapsychology Foundation, 1964).

Edward F. Domino, Editor, *PCP, Historical and Current Perspectives* (Ann Arbor: NPP Books, 1981).

Ronald L. Linden, *PCP, The Devil's Dust: Recognition, Management, and Prevention of Phencyclidine Abuse* (Belmont, CA: Wadsworth Publication Co., 1981).

Tips for Teens About Inhalants (Rockville, Md: Center for Substance Abuse Prevention, 1994).

John Kaplan, *The Hardest Drug: Heroin and Public Policy* (Chicago: University of Chicago Press, 1983).

www.stopdrugs.com

www.dancesafe.com

www.resort.com/~banshee/Info/N20/nitrous.dangers/html

ABOUT THE AUTHOR

Passionate in her experiences both personal and professional, Jessica Lohman became captivated by drug education at an early age. An enthusiastic classroom presenter on the topic of drug awareness, her background includes working with the California Department of Justice and participating as an active member of the law enforcement community. She has been known to identify with teen issues and tirelessly advocate for the success of young people while maintaining as an integral leader in partner collaboration between community agencies.